Let Freedom Ring

The Battle
of Yorktown

By Dee Ready

Consultant:
Edward Ayres
Historian, Yorktown Victory Center
Jamestown-Yorktown Foundation
Williamsburg, Virginia

Bridgestone Books
an imprint of Capstone Press
Mankato, Minnesota

Bridgestone Books are published by Capstone Press,
151 Good Counsel Drive • P.O. Box 669 • Mankato, Minnesota 56002.
www.capstonepress.com

Printed in the United States of America

Library of Congress Cataloging-in-Publication Data
Ready, Dee.
  The Battle of Yorktown / by Dee Ready.
    p. cm. — (Let freedom ring)
  Includes bibliographical references and index.
  ISBN 0-7368-1097-8 (hardcover)
  ISBN 0-7368-4490-2 (paperback)
  1. Yorktown (Va.)—History—Siege, 1781—Juvenile literature. [1. Yorktown (Va.)—
History—Siege, 1781 2. United States—History—Revolution, 1775–1783—Campaigns.]
I. Title. II. Series.
E241.Y6 R43 2002
973.3'37—dc21   2001005005

Summary: Details the last major battle of the American Revolution—the Battle of Yorktown,
    which brought victory to the American Patriots. Discusses how America and Britain came
    to war, the role of the French, and some of the other battles fought.

Editorial Credits
Rebecca Aldridge, editor; Kia Bielke, cover designer, interior layout designer, and interior
illustrator; Jennifer Schonborn, cover production designer; Jo Miller, photo researcher

Photo Credits
Cover: CORBIS; North Wind Picture Archives, 5, 7, 12, 15, 23, 27, 31, 35, 36, 42;
Bettmann/CORBIS, 11, 39; Hulton/Archive Photos, 16, 25, 28, 40–41; Index Stock
Imagery/James Lemass, 19; Scala/Art Resource, NY, 21; The Granger Collection, New York,
24; Giraudon/Art Resource, NY, 32

1   2   3   4   5   6   07   06   05   04   03   02

Table of Contents

Chapter One

An End and Its Beginning

Cannons boomed and balls from guns called muskets zoomed through the air. American and French soldiers heard the faint sound of a drumbeat. On the top of a hill stood a young drummer dressed in the red coat of a British soldier. He beat out a message on his drum. Slowly, the American and French soldiers lowered their weapons and stopped firing their cannons. The soldiers listened to the drum. It meant the British wanted a meeting.

A British officer walked through the gun smoke rising in the air. He waved a white cloth, a signal that he came in peace. The officer had a message for General George Washington, leader of the Continental Army. American soldiers blindfolded the officer and marched him to Washington's tent. There he told the American general that Lord Charles Cornwallis, the British commander, wanted to surrender.

The day was October 17, 1781, and the Battle of Yorktown was over.

Two British soldiers, one drumming and one waving a white flag, signaled the end of the Battle of Yorktown.

What Yorktown Was Like

Yorktown, Virginia, was a small but busy seaport in 1781. Along the waterfront were docks and places to repair ships. A ferryboat went between Yorktown and Gloucester, Virginia, a town right across the York River.

Yorktown was established in the 1690s and soon became an important center for the tobacco and slave trade in Virginia. Tobacco earned more money than any other item that Virginia sold to Britain.

But how did the battle in this small southern village begin?

The French and Indian War

When colonists first came to America, they were a proud part of the British Empire. But the French and Indian War (1754–1763) brought change.

At that time, each of the 13 colonies had a militia. These men trained in their villages as soldiers to fight in emergencies. Militiamen from

many of the colonies fought side by side with British soldiers in the war against France and its American Indian friends. With the help of the colonial militias, the British won the French and Indian War. With the French defeated, the colonists believed that they could take care of themselves.

Britain Begins to Tax the Colonists

After the French and Indian War, Britain was in great debt. King George III of Britain felt that the

Parliament began to tax the colonists to help pay Britain's debt after the French and Indian War.

colonists should help pay this debt. After all, the British had protected the colonists during the war. The debt belonged to them, too. So in 1764, Parliament, Britain's lawmaking body, began to tax the colonists.

Over the next several years, Parliament passed a number of laws that were unpopular in the colonies. The Sugar Act raised taxes on molasses entering the colonies from non-British ports. The Stamp Act taxed various pieces of printed materials such as newspapers, legal documents, and even playing cards. The Townshend Acts taxed glass, lead paint, paper, and tea when they arrived in the colonies.

To all these taxes, colonists said, "No taxation without representation!" They believed that Britain had no right to tax them because the colonies had no one representing them in Parliament. To protest, the colonists stopped buying taxed goods. This boycott made Parliament and King George angry. The trouble between Britain and the 13 colonies was just beginning.

CANADA

The Great Lakes Region

St. Lawrence River

NEW HAMPSHIRE

(District of Maine)

MASSACHUSETTS

NEW YORK

New York City

Boston

RHODE ISLAND

Newport

PENNSYLVANIA

CONNECTICUT

NEW JERSEY

DELAWARE

MARYLAND

Mississippi River

VIRGINIA

Yorktown

NORTH CAROLINA

SOUTH CAROLINA

GEORGIA

Charleston

Savannah

ATLANTIC OCEAN

Miles

0 50 100 150 200

0 100 200 300

Kilometers

N *E* *W* *S*

The 13 Colonies in 1764

Chapter Two

The Start of War

Colonial protest worked, and by March 1770, Parliament erased all but one tax in the colonies— the tax on tea. The tea tax cost colonists only a few pennies each year. However, Parliament controlled the sale of tea. Colonists thought that if the British government could control the selling of tea, it could take control of all trade in the 13 colonies. In protest, colonists boycotted tea shipped from Britain.

On December 16, 1773, colonial men boarded three British tea ships and dumped their loads of tea into Boston Harbor. When news of this Boston Tea Party reached Britain, Parliament closed down the port of Boston. Ships could not sail into or out of Boston Harbor to sell goods. Other people in the 13 colonies sent goods and money to help Boston.

The First Battle

The colonies tried to settle their differences with Britain peacefully. In 1774, leaders from

In December 1773, three ships loaded with tea docked in Boston Harbor. On December 16, colonial men upset with British laws boarded each of the tea ships and dumped the tea into the harbor (above).

12 of the 13 colonies met in the First Continental Congress. These leaders sent a letter to Britain. It stated colonists' reasons for opposing taxation without representation. The letter only made King George III angrier.

In April 1775, Parliament told the governor of Massachusetts to put a stop to the colonists' activities there. Colonists had begun buying and storing weapons for a possible fight with Britain. On

On July 2, 1775, 43-year-old George Washington rode into the Patriot camp in Massachusetts. There, he took command of what was now called the Continental Army. The men who were gathered at the camp cheered their new general's arrival. They were ready to fight.

the night of April 18, 1775, British soldiers left Boston and marched toward Concord. The soldiers had orders to find the stored weapons.

When British soldiers arrived in Lexington, a town on the route to Concord, they faced militia members who were ready and waiting. Someone fired a shot, and fighting broke out. Eight militiamen died. The British marched on to Concord, where more lives, both American and British, were lost. America's Revolutionary War had begun.

The Second Continental Congress

Colonial leaders met for a second time on May 10, 1775. This Second Continental Congress planned for war. The leaders sent another letter to Britain's king. They asked him to recognize their right to make their own laws and collect their own taxes. King George III refused to listen, and the war between the colonies and Britain continued.

The Second Continental Congress also chose a leader for all the colonial troops. They selected George Washington, a man who had proved himself a skilled leader in the French and Indian War.

Chapter Three

The Two Armies

When Washington arrived in Massachusetts, he found a large group of soldiers with little formal training. Just a few days before, they had been simple farmers and merchants. They were not as well trained as the British soldiers, but they were willing to learn.

Strengths and Weaknesses of the Patriots

The Continental Army had several strengths. First, it had a good leader in General George Washington. He believed in independence, the cause for which he was fighting. Many of the officers and soldiers in his army believed in the cause as well. Second, some colonists had already fought in the French and Indian War. These men knew how to use muskets. Third, the Continental Army had the advantage of fighting on its own land.

But the Continental Army had many challenges, too. The first challenge was that the Continental Congress had little

The image above shows how a soldier in the Continental Army may have dressed. Many Continental Army soldiers had little formal military training.

money with which to pay the American soldiers. Congress had little money to buy food, clothing, and ammunition for them, either. In fact, Congress depended on several European countries to provide these military supplies. A weak American navy was another challenge facing the colonists.

Washington had two kinds of soldiers, which brought more challenges. The first type of soldier belonged to the Continental Army. The second kind of fighter belonged to militias from the states. Many

This document, which George Washington signed, gives instructions for enlisting men into the Continental Army.

of the militias did not have good leaders. Militiamen often ran from battle when British soldiers started firing. These facts made winning battles hard for Washington.

Many soldiers enlisted, or signed up to fight, for only a few months. When their time was up, they went home. So Washington's army sometimes had as many as 15,000 soldiers in it. Other times it had only 3,000 men. Whenever the American army won a battle, however, many more colonists joined and became soldiers.

One problem for the Continental Army came from among the colonists themselves. As many as one of every three colonists supported the British. These people, called Loyalists or Tories, refused to help the Patriots and sometimes spied for the British.

Strengths and Weaknesses of the British

The British army had a lot going for it. British soldiers had trained together for months, sometimes years. Their weapons and equipment were the best available. The British army had well-trained leaders, as well as warm clothes and good food.

Help for Washington's Men

During the winter of 1777–1778 at Valley Forge, Pennsylvania, Washington's troops suffered from hunger and cold. But something good came out of that time. Baron Friedrich von Steuben from Prussia in Europe came to Valley Forge and offered to train the colonial soldiers.

Von Steuben drilled the men. He taught them to fight, march, and obey commands like British soldiers. Von Steuben gave Washington new hope that winter. In the spring of 1778, Washington and his men went on to a victory at Monmouth Court House in New Jersey.

Unlike the Continental Congress, the British Parliament had money. It could hire soldiers from other European countries to fight in its army. It did hire 30,000 soldiers from Hesse, in Germany. These Hessians fought for Britain.

Besides having well-trained soldiers, Britain had a strong navy. The British also had the help of Tories in many of the colonies.

But the British army did have its weaknesses. British soldiers were not used to the kind of fighting that Americans had learned during the French and Indian War. British soldiers had to fight far from their homeland and their loved ones. They had little to fight for. Britain was also fighting other wars in Europe. So Parliament could not send all of its soldiers to the colonies.

Life of a British Soldier

Britain had an army of professional soldiers, not a militia. Soldiers (like the ones shown in the modern-day reenactment below) joined the army, and it became their life. Many soldiers enlisted to get out of jail. Soldiers had to be careful. The army might hang them for more than 200 reasons, ranging from acting against Britain to stealing a loaf of bread.

A British soldier needed three hours to get dressed because he had to brush all the dirt off his uniform. On a march, he carried more than 60 pounds (27 kilograms) of equipment, including a 14-pound (6-kilogram) musket.

A British soldier who was not an officer earned eight pence a day. That would be two cents in today's U.S. money. He had to buy his own shoes, socks, medicine, and gloves. He also had to pay for repairing his musket.

Chapter Four

Fighting for Independence

During the first year of the war, colonists had different reasons for fighting. Some just wanted the British to treat them fairly. Others wanted independence. On July 4, 1776, the members of the Second Continental Congress issued an important document, the Declaration of Independence. It stated that the 13 colonies were "free and independent states." The Continental Army fought to make the words become true. If the army won the war, the colonies would be free from Britain.

War Goes On

From 1775 to 1777, both Britain and America had victories. Both sides also suffered defeat. The Continental Army lost the Battle of Bunker Hill in June 1775 when the Patriots ran out of ammunition. In the spring of 1776, Patriots seized Dorchester Heights, a tall hill that looked down on Boston. In August 1776, British troops defeated the Americans in

The Battle of Bunker Hill

On June 17, 1775, approximately 2,500 British soldiers attacked Patriots on a hill overlooking Boston Harbor. The British troops prepared to fight with the knifelike bayonets on the end of their muskets. They were easy targets for the Americans, and many British soldiers fell. The British charged a second time. Again, the Patriots forced them back. The British attacked a third time. The Patriots ran out of ammunition, so they threw stones at the British.

The Patriots proved they could fight but lost this battle to the British. This Battle of Bunker Hill (right) marked the second battle of the Revolutionary War.

FLAGS IN AMERICA'S HISTORY

THE BATTLE OF BUNKER HILL

The Bunker Hill flag is representative of the "pine tree flags," of which there were many in the early days of the American Revolution . . . before an official flag had been designated for the Colonial armies. The pine tree was the emblem of the Massachusetts Bay Colony, proclaiming simply, but with native dignity, the colonist's love for the pine-clad hills of his new homeland. The Bunker Hill flag was made from the old blue English Ensign, with its red St. George's cross, by inserting a pine tree in the upper left quarter of the canton.

The painting shows the Colonials in the trenches at Bunker Hill, ready to resist the attack of the English Grenadiers. Striding through the trench can be seen Colonel Prescott, who gave the famous order, "Don't fire until you see the whites of their eyes." The moral effects of this battle were inestimable, for two attacks were repulsed with heavy enemy losses before the Colonials, their ammunition depleted, were dislodged. It dispelled the almost superstitious belief in the impossibility of encountering regular troops with volunteers.

THE BUNKER HILL FLAG

A Spy for Washington

In late August 1776, the Americans lost the Battle of Long Island. To hold on to New York City, General Washington needed information about what the British were doing on Long Island. Captain Nathan Hale, who had been a schoolteacher, volunteered to find out.

While Hale was on his spying mission, the British captured and hanged him. Witnesses said that Hale's last words were: "I only regret that I have but one life to lose for my country." Hale was only 21 years old.

New York. In 1776, Continental soldiers won winter victories in Trenton and Princeton, New Jersey. The Continental Army lost at Brandywine and Germantown, Pennsylvania, in 1777.

The year 1778 dragged on with more wins and losses for the Continental Army. During that time, Washington led his troops to White Plains, New York. From there, he hoped to keep the British in New York City. From 1778 to 1781, Washington kept his troops in New York and surrounded the British army stationed there.

France Enters the War

For many hundreds of years, France and Britain had fought one another. The Continental Congress had always hoped that France would enter the war and help the Continental Army fight

Britain. Congress wanted France to send soldiers, ships, and money to the colonies.

In October 1777, American soldiers defeated the British at Saratoga, New York. This victory led France to promise in February 1778 that it would enter the war and help the colonies. However, many months passed, and France did nothing.

In July 1780, the Comte Jean-Baptiste de Rochambeau arrived from France with 5,000 soldiers. They camped in Newport, Rhode Island, for about one year. Rochambeau told Washington

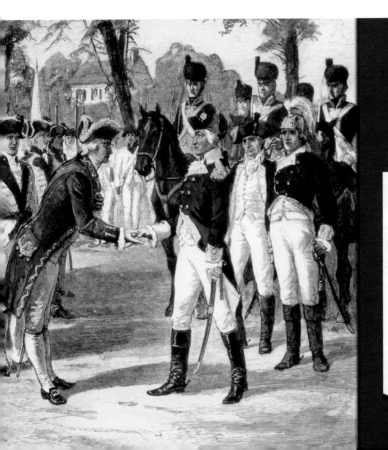

Rochambeau (bowing) and his soldiers joined Washington (shaking Rochambeau's hand) and soldiers of the Continental Army.

that the American general could command him and all his French troops.

Washington knew how helpful a French soldier could be. In 1777, the 20-year-old Marquis de Lafayette had sailed across the Atlantic because he so admired Washington. Lafayette had ignored French officials to join the Continental Army as a major general.

After the Revolutionary War, Lafayette returned to France a hero. He came back to America in 1784 and stayed with Washington and his wife, Martha. Lafayette received a hero's welcome when he came to America again in 1824. When he returned to France, he took some American soil with him. This soil was used to bury him after his death in 1834.

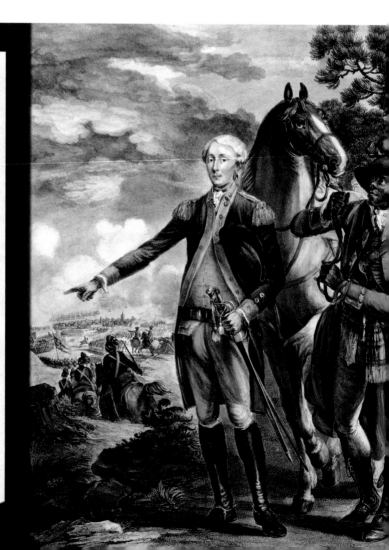

Help for American Prisoners

During the war, the British captured many American soldiers. They imprisoned some of them in ships in New York Harbor. The soldiers suffered greatly on these boats. The British packed as many as 1,100 prisoners in each ship. Crowded together, they had little food. They risked being hanged if they complained. More than 7,000 American soldiers died on these prison ships.

Elizabeth Burgin lived in New York City. She often visited the prison ships and brought food to the American soldiers held on them. A Patriot officer asked for her help in getting prisoners off the ships. With several other women, Burgin got word to the prisoners and helped more than 200 escape. Later, she herself had to escape when the British offered a big reward for her capture.

Chapter Five

Hope Lies in the South

While Washington and Rochambeau remained outside New York City, the British made their own plans. They decided that if they could not win in the North, they would win in the South. With a strong navy, the British could sail down the Atlantic Coast and attack seacoast cities in the southern colonies.

In 1778, the British attacked and captured Savannah, Georgia. In 1780, they captured Charleston, South Carolina. They quickly gained control of Georgia and South Carolina. With these victories, the British could move north through the southern colonies.

Southern Patriots did everything they could to keep the British from taking control of North Carolina and moving into Virginia. They beat the British in several battles, causing British General Charles Cornwallis to give up on North Carolina. He headed instead to Virginia with about 8,000 troops, arriving in May 1781.

General Charles Cornwallis

Cornwallis understood why the colonists were upset with Britain. In 1766, as a member of Parliament, he voted against the Declaratory Act. This law stated that Britain had the right to determine taxes in the colonies. Cornwallis still accepted command of troops in North America once the Revolutionary War began.

Nathanael Greene

Major General Nathanael Greene led many small battles against the British throughout the South. Greene was born the son of a Quaker. Quakers are peaceful people with strong faith in God. They oppose war and refuse to carry guns. Greene was forced to leave the Quakers in 1773 because he had attended a military parade.

Washington sent Lafayette and 1,200 soldiers south to keep the British from causing trouble in Virginia. Cornwallis spent two months destroying military supplies. He even tried unsuccessfully to capture Governor Thomas Jefferson. Lafayette did not have enough men to fight a major battle, but he did prevent the British from doing much damage.

Cornwallis Occupies Yorktown

By August, Cornwallis decided to allow his tired soldiers to rest at Yorktown, Virginia, a town surrounded by water on three sides. Cornwallis thought that this location would help keep his troops safe from an American army attack.

Cornwallis also expected the British commander in New York, Henry Clinton, to send ships to protect his soldiers. These ships would bring more British troops, as well as ammunition and supplies. Cornwallis believed that he could then defeat any number of Continental soldiers.

To assure victory, Cornwallis built trenches in the land around Yorktown. These long ditches had steep banks that let soldiers hide in them. Also, Cornwallis built forts of earth surrounded by sharpened logs. In these redoubts, Cornwallis placed cannons. He believed that his troops were now ready for any attack by land.

Good News

Lafayette told Washington that Cornwallis's army was in Yorktown. Washington had to decide to attack New York as planned or go south. Rochambeau favored marching south toward Yorktown.

Washington then received an important letter from Admiral the Comte de Grasse. He commanded the French fleet in the West Indies, islands south and east of Florida. In his letter, de Grasse promised to bring his fleet of 28 ships to Chesapeake Bay near Yorktown at the end of August. He planned to stay there until October, when weather would force his ships south again.

During those weeks, de Grasse would be glad to help the Continental Army. Washington had thought de Grasse would bring his fleet to New York. With this new information, Washington immediately made plans to head south.

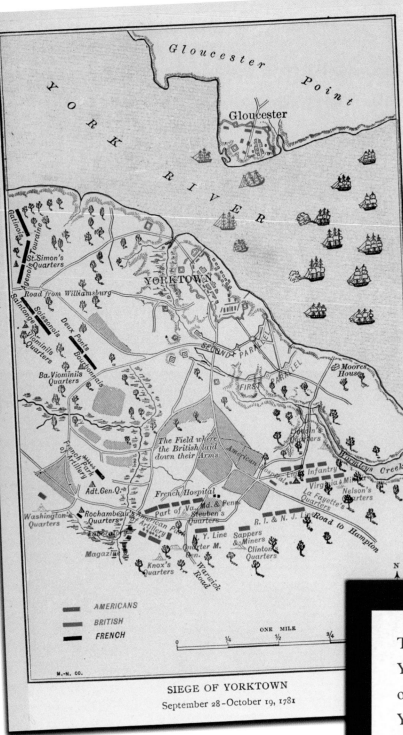

YORKTOWN

Road from Williamsburg

SECOND PARALLEL

FIRST PARALLEL

Moores House

The Field where the British laid down their Arms

Wormley's Creek

French park of Artillery

Adt. Gen. Q.

French Hospital

Infantry

Virginia & Md.

Nelson's Quarters

La Fayette's Quarters

Washington's Quarters

Rochambeau's Quarters

American Park of Artillery

part of Va.

Md. & Penn

Steuben's Quarters

R. I. & N. J. Line Road to Hampton

N. Y. Line

Sappers & Miners

Clinton Quarters

Road to Hampton

Magazine

Knox's Quarters

Quarter M. Gen.

Warwick Road

N

Gloucester Point

Gloucester

YORK RIVER

YORK

Ratineau's

St. Simon's Quarters

Agenois

Saintonge

Soissonais

Viominil's Quarters

Deux Ponts

Bourbonnais

Ba. Viominil's Quarters

Logan Quarters

American Hospital

AMERICANS
BRITISH
FRENCH

ONE MILE
0   1/4   1/2   3/4

M.-N. CO.

SIEGE OF YORKTOWN
September 28-October 19, 1781

This map illustrates Yorktown and the town of Gloucester across the York River.

The Continental Army Heads South

On August 19, 1781, Washington and Rochambeau led nearly 7,000 Continental and French soldiers out of New York. They left about 3,000 soldiers in New York to try to fool the British. If the British still saw American and French troops in the city, they might not know what the Americans had planned.

On September 1, the American and French troops marched through Philadelphia, Pennsylvania. It was not until September 2 that British General

De Grasse's fleet drove off 19 British ships within days of its arrival at Chesapeake Bay. The British ships headed back to New York.

Henry Clinton learned that Washington and Rochambeau were on the move. Once Clinton learned of the marching troops, he warned Cornwallis of their approach.

During the march, Washington worried that the British navy might arrive at Chesapeake Bay before de Grasse and his ships got there. If they did, Cornwallis would have help. But de Grasse could trap Cornwallis at Yorktown if he got there before Clinton's troops did.

On September 4, Washington learned that de Grasse was at Chesapeake Bay with 3,000 French troops. The British fleet arrived the next day. On September 16, Washington got word that the French fleet had driven off the British ships. Washington knew that de Grasse had trapped Cornwallis.

The March

The distance from New York to Yorktown was about 500 miles (805 kilometers). The French and American troops marched about 15 miles (24 kilometers) per day. Moving an army in the 1780s was not easy. Few bridges existed, and roads were little more than trails. Finding enough food along the way to feed the men and animals was hard.

Chapter Six

The Siege of Yorktown

During the next few weeks, Washington and Rochambeau's troops began to arrive in the area around Yorktown. Lafayette and his soldiers joined them. By October 1781, almost 20,000 American and French troops were in place and ready to fight.

The Siege Begins

On October 6, American and French soldiers began building trenches about 800 yards (730 meters) away from the British lines. About 1,000 soldiers could fire cannons from the trenches at the British.

On October 9, the battle began when the French fired cannons at the town. Washington and Rochambeau knew that this battle would last more than a single day. It would be a siege. The Americans and the French would surround the town until the British surrendered.

George Washington himself fired the first American cannon toward
Yorktown on October 9, 1781.

The Patriots Move Closer

By October 11, colonial and French soldiers were shelling Yorktown with more than 50 cannons. That night, the soldiers dug a trench even closer to the British, less than 400 yards (366 meters) away. It took two days to move all the weapons into this new trench. This close, the cannons could hardly miss their target when fired.

On October 14, Washington ordered an attack on two British redoubts separated from the town's main defenses. French soldiers attacked one and

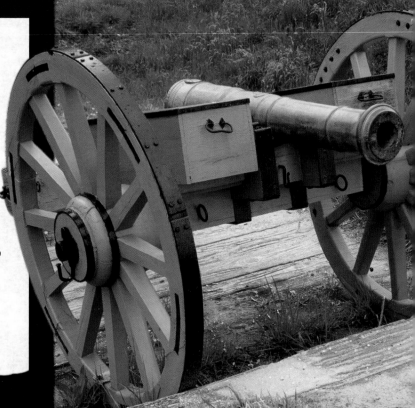

At the Battle of Yorktown, cannons like the one at right were used. The British killed 83 French and American soldiers and wounded 258. The combined American and French troops killed 156 British soldiers and wounded 326.

captured it. Lieutenant Colonel Alexander Hamilton and his men attacked the other redoubt. Hamilton told his soldiers not to load their guns. Using only the bayonets at the end of their muskets, Hamilton and his men captured the redoubt. The next day, the Patriots began extending their trenches to these redoubts. The Americans and the French were even closer to the British. They could fire cannons into almost any part of the city.

Two days later, Cornwallis sent some of his troops to attack the French. But his troops quickly failed and turned back. That night, Cornwallis tried to escape with his army. They planned to cross the York River into Gloucester. From there, they would march to the safety of New York. One group of troops made it across the river. But a sudden storm swept down, making escape impossible for Cornwallis and the rest of his men.

Cornwallis Gives Up

During the night and in the early morning hours of October 17, 1781, American and French troops continued firing at Yorktown. The British redoubts and trenches around Yorktown crumbled. Cornwallis

Surrender of the British

"Several flags pass and repass now even without the drum. Had we not seen the drummer in his red coat when he first mounted, he might have beat away till doomsday. The constant firing was too much for the sound of a single drum. But when the firing ceased, I thought I never heard a drum equal to it—the most delightful music to us all."
—19-year-old soldier Ebenezer Denny in his war diary dated October 18, 1781

knew he could not outlast the siege. Admiral de Grasse's French ships had kept food and ammunition from reaching Yorktown.

Later that morning, Cornwallis sent two soldiers. One soldier drummed while the other waved a white cloth of surrender. Officers from both sides met to discuss terms. They agreed that the British army would surrender to the Americans. The navy would surrender to the French. British officers would be able to keep their swords and personal property. Cornwallis and a few other British officers would be allowed to return to Britain. The other British soldiers would be prisoners in America.

The Surrender Ceremony

On October 19, American soldiers lined up on one side of a road leading out of Yorktown. The French lined up on the other side. British soldiers marched down the road between these two lines and laid down their muskets.

Cornwallis, embarrassed by the Patriot and French victory, sent his second-in-command, Charles O'Hara, to the

". . . the British officers in general behaved like boys who had been whipped at school. Some bit their lips; some pouted; others cried. Their round, broad-rimmed hats were well-adapted to the occasion, hiding those faces they were ashamed to show."
—a New Jersey officer speaking about the surrender ceremony at Yorktown (shown here)

ceremony. To mark the surrender, O'Hara delivered Cornwallis's sword to the Americans and French. O'Hara tried to give the sword to Rochambeau, but the French commander sent O'Hara to George Washington. Washington pointed O'Hara toward Major General Benjamin Lincoln, General Washington's second-in-command. O'Hara gave Lincoln the sword.

Legend says the British war prisoners marched out of Yorktown to "The World Turned Upside Down." This song included words such as:

*If ponies rode men and grass
ate cows,
And cats were chased into
holes by the mouse . . .
If summer were spring and
the other way round,
Then all the world would be
upside down.*

This song represented how the British felt. British soldiers could not believe that they had lost to the Americans.

A Free Nation

Although some small fights occurred after Yorktown, this final big battle of the Revolutionary War had ended. The Patriots, with the help of the French, had won.

The American victory at Yorktown led the British Parliament and King George III to give up the fight. In April 1782, representatives from Britain, the United States, and France met in Paris to talk about peace. On September 3, 1783, the representatives signed the Treaty of Paris and ended the Revolutionary War. The United States was a free and independent nation.

This image shows the signing of the Treaty of Paris in 1783. The treaty officially ended the Revolutionary War.

TIMELINE

The French and Indian War begins. It ends in 1763.

Parliament passes the Townshend Acts.

British Parliament passes the Sugar Act.

The Battles of Lexington and Concord start the Revolutionary War; General George Washington takes command of the Continental Army.

Parliament passes the Stamp Act.

| 1754 | 1764 | 1765 | 1767 | 1773 | 1775 |

The Boston Tea Party takes place.

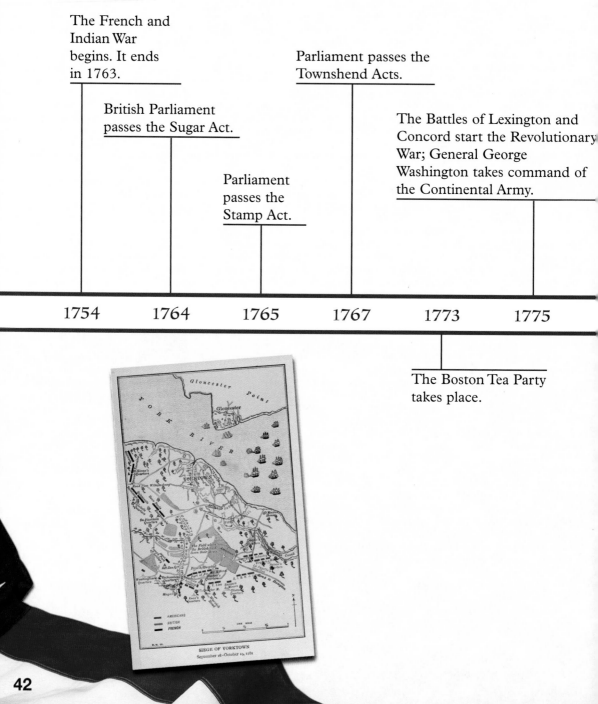

SIEGE OF YORKTOWN
September 28–October 19, 1781

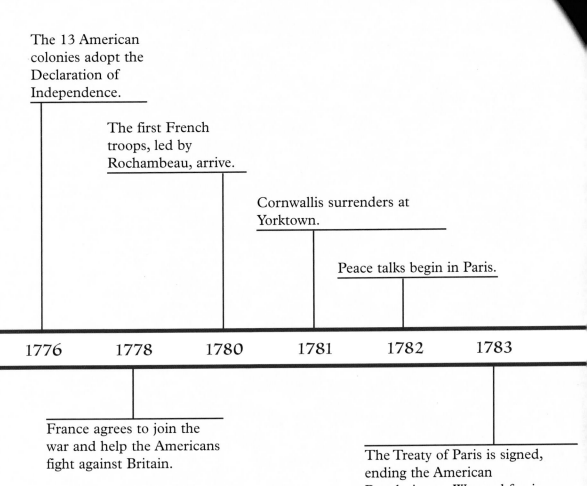

The 13 American colonies adopt the Declaration of Independence.

The first French troops, led by Rochambeau, arrive.

Cornwallis surrenders at Yorktown.

Peace talks begin in Paris.

1776   1778   1780   1781   1782   1783

France agrees to join the war and help the Americans fight against Britain.

The Treaty of Paris is signed, ending the American Revolutionary War and freeing the colonies from Britain.

Glossary

boycott (BOI-kot)—to refuse to buy certain goods as a means of protest

Loyalist (LOI-uh-list)—a colonist who sided with the British during the Revolutionary War

militia (muh-LISH-uh)—a group of people trained to fight but who serve only in times of emergency

militiamen (muh-LISH-uh-men)—volunteer soldiers in the American Revolution served only in emergency situations

musket (MUHSS-kit)—a gun with a long barrel

Parliament (PAR-luh-muhnt)—Britain's governing body of lawmakers

Patriot (PAY-tree-uht)—a colonist loyal to America during the Revolutionary War; Patriots wanted to form a new nation independent of Britain.

redoubt (ri-DOUT)—a small fort that is built to last for only a short time

representation (rep-ri-zen-TAY-shuhn)—an elected body that acts for others in government

revolution (rev-uh-LOO-shuhn)—an uprising that attempts to change a way of government

siege (SEEJ)—a military move in which one army surrounds another and keeps supplies and food from getting to the second army, forcing its surrender

Tory (TOR-ee)—another name for a Loyalist

For Further Reading

Collier, Christopher, and James Lincoln Collier. *The American Revolution: 1763–1783.* The Drama of American History. New York: Benchmark Books, 1998.

Gourley, Catherine. *Welcome to Felicity's World, 1774.* The American Girls Collection. Middleton, Wis.: Pleasant Company Publications, 1999.

Hakim, Joy. *From Colonies to Country.* History of US. New York: Oxford University Press, 1999.

Silcox-Jarrett, Diane. *Heroines of the American Revolution: America's Founding Mothers.* Heroines of History. Chapel Hill, N.C.: Green Angel Press, 1998.

Todd, Anne. *The Revolutionary War.* America Goes to War. Mankato, Minn.: Capstone Books, 2001.

Weber, Michael. *Yorktown.* Battlefields across America. New York: Twenty-First Century Books, 1997.

Places of Interest

**Colonial National
Historical Park**
P.O. Box 210
Yorktown, VA 23690-0210
*http://www.nps.gov/colo/home.
htm*
Site includes Yorktown and
its battlefield

**Fort Necessity
National Battlefield**
One Washington Parkway
Farmington, PA 15437
*http://www.nps.gov/fone/home.
htm*
The site of the first battle of the
French and Indian War

**Saratoga National
Historical Park**
648 Route 32
Stillwater, NY 12170
*http://www.nps.gov/sara/f-sara.
htm*
Battlefield of the turning point of
the Revolutionary War

**Valley Forge
National Historical Park**
P.O. Box 953
Valley Forge, PA 19482-0953
*http://www.nps.gov/vafo/home.
htm*
Where General Washington and
his men camped during the
winter of 1777–1778; also where
Prussia's Baron Friedrich von
Steuben trained members of the
colonial army.

Yorktown Victory Center
Route 238: Colonial Parkway
Yorktown, VA 23690
*http://www.historyisfun.org/
jyf1/yvc.html*
A gallery and living history
museum dedicated to the last
major battle of the American
Revolutionary War

Internet Sites

Do you want to learn more about The Battle of Yorktown?
Visit the FactHound at *www.facthound.com*

FactHound can track down many sites to help you. All the
FactHound sites are hand-selected by our editors. FactHound will
fetch the best, most accurate information to answer your questions.

IT'S EASY! IT'S FUN!
1) Go to *www.facthound.com*
2) Type in: **0736810978**
3) Click on **FETCH IT** and FactHound will put you on the trail
   of several helpful links.

You can also search by subject or book title. So, relax
and let our pal FactHound do the research for you!

Index